# SHAW'S FORTUNE

# SHAW'S FORTUNE

## The Picture Story of a Colonial Plantation

*Drawn
and Written by*

# EDWIN TUNIS

THE WORLD PUBLISHING COMPANY

*Cleveland and New York*

*Books by Edwin Tunis*

SHAW'S FORTUNE

COLONIAL CRAFTSMEN

FRONTIER LIVING

INDIANS

COLONIAL LIVING

WHEELS

WEAPONS

OARS, SAILS AND STEAM

Library of Congress catalog card number: AC 66-10646
HL 66

Published by The World Publishing Company
2231 West 110th Street, Cleveland, Ohio 44102

Published simultaneously in Canada by
Nelson, Foster & Scott Ltd.

1788
Grandfather's
Grandfather's
Grandfather

1650
Alan Shaw

1920
Grandfather

1620
Bart Andrews
the oronooko

1752
Malcolm Shaw

1854
Grandfather's
Grandfather

More than 350 years ago, in 1607, a group of English adventurers settled Jamestown, near the Chesapeake Bay, in Virginia. The town lasted almost a hundred years, long enough to be called the first permanent English settlement. James the First was King of England in 1607 and he was also King of America. He, and the kings who followed him, ruled the colonies for 169 years. This book is about the way people lived then around the Chesapeake Bay.

The first part of the book tells how the plantations started and how things were on one particular plantation not long after Jamestown was settled. That was more than a hundred years before your grandfather's grandfather's grandfather was born. The rest of the book tells about the same plantation as it was in 1752. Things had changed a lot. George Washington was twenty that year. He had just inherited Mt. Vernon from his brother, Lawrence.

*The oronooko's plantation*

The American Indians grew tobacco but it was so bitter that they couldn't smoke it unless they mixed willow bark or sumac leaves with it. Europeans hated it. They liked the mild tobacco that the Spanish brought from South America. This they called "oronooko" because it came from the Orinoco River. People didn't spell very well in those days.

One of the Jamestown adventurers was John Rolfe. He is famous because he married Pocahontas, the Indian "princess." But he did something else that was more important. He managed to get some seeds of mild oronooko and plant them in Virginia. The settlers never found the gold they looked for but this tobacco was another kind of gold—they could sell it in England. So every man dropped what he was doing and started growing tobacco. They even grew it in the streets of Jamestown. They grew so much of it that they didn't have time to grow food and sometimes they went hungry. That soon taught them not to overdo things.

More and more people came to Virginia and Maryland and made clearings in the forest for tobacco. They called the clearings plantations. When a man moved on to new land, he didn't cut the trees down, he killed them by cutting through their bark all the way around their trunks. This let in sunlight, and he planted his first crop between the dead trees. A planter on such a small clearing was called an "oronooko" after the kind of tobacco he grew. He lived in a hut while he hewed timbers out of some of the trees to build himself a cabin. He split rough boards from logs and used them to cover the outside of the cabin. He thatched its steep roof with rushes. For a chimney, he piled long "loaves" of wet clay, called "cats," one on another, around the four sides. He placed a wooden pole at each of the chimney's four corners to help it stand up.

The oronooko put the doorway of his house at one end of

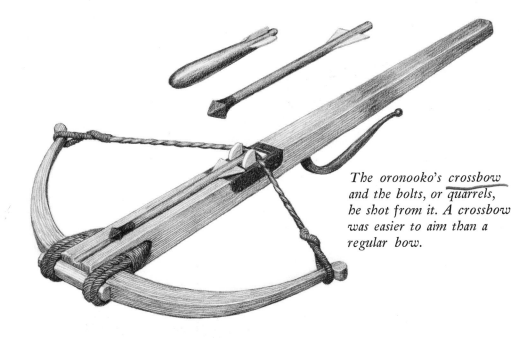

*The oronooko's crossbow and the bolts, or quarrels, he shot from it. A crossbow was easier to aim than a regular bow.*

the front wall. He built the door of heavy planks and made a strong wooden bar to put across it at night because you never knew what the Indians might do. His windows were small and there were only two or three of them for the whole house. He had no glass, so he used oiled paper, if he could get it, or rabbit skin with the hair scraped off. You couldn't see through such windows but they let in a little light. Wooden shutters covered the insides of the windows at night.

These small planters often moved on to new land when too many crops ruined their old land. When a man did this he usually burned down his house to get the nails from it for a new one. All nails were handmade and hard to get. The Virginia colony offered to give any man enough nails for a house if he would leave his old one standing for someone else.

*Inside the cabin*

What little furniture the oronooko had in his cabin was rough stuff he made himself: a long table and a couple of benches made of split logs, flat side up. If he had a bed, it was no more than a low platform built in one corner of the room. Its mattress was stuffed with rushes or dry leaves. The boys in the family slept in the space under the roof and climbed a ladder to get there. Usually everybody went to bed when darkness fell. The fire gave a little light. If he needed more, the oronooko lit a grease lamp called a "cruse." It was a dish with a lip like that of a pitcher. The dish held grease; a wick burned in the lip and dripped, and smoked, and smelled bad.

Packed clay made a good enough floor for most cabins, but some had "puncheon floors" made of half-logs flat side up like the ones used for benches. When he had time to do it, the planter sawed boards from logs and covered the inside walls of his house with them.

The oronooko's wife did her cooking in the fireplace over the open fire. This wasn't unusual; it was the way everybody cooked then. The family ate their food from trenchers. These were flat slabs of wood hollowed out a little. Some of the food they ate was wild game that the oronooko shot with a crossbow. Soldiers had guns but they weren't much good for hunting. By the time you got the "match" burning and persuaded the gun to go off, the game had left.

*A trencher and a cruse*

9

Most of the plantations were small at first, but some men with enough money started larger ones. The large ones bought up the small ones and became still larger. Before the end of a hundred years the large plantations had most of the best flat land near the Bay. The small ones were pushed back.

Alan Shaw grew up in Scotland and married Margaret Duncan there. With a little money and a lot of ambition, Alan and Meg came to America. Here they bought a piece of land from an oronooko named Andrews, who was moving. The land lay near the head of Manokin Bay, a small inlet of the Chesapeake.

After twenty years of hard work Alan and Meg had a successful plantation. They named it Shaw's Fortune.

Alan owned some Negro slaves who worked his fields. He also had workers called bond servants. These English men and women were too poor to pay their way to America, so Master Shaw paid for their passage. Then they worked for him for four or five years, without any wages, to pay him back. He fed them and clothed them. At the end of their term he gave them some corn and some new clothes, and they were free.

With all this help, Alan Shaw made bricks and built a fairly

10

comfortable house. It wasn't very large but it was the largest on the place, so it was called the "Big House." It was two stories high, with a steep shingled roof, Big chimneys stood at both of its end walls. The ground floor was divided into two rooms, the hall and the parlor. Above these were two bedrooms. Each of the four rooms had a fireplace. A narrow stair led from the hall to the bedroom above it.

The windows of the Big House had glass in them. This glass was set in the window frames corner up, so that the small square panes appeared to be diamond shaped. Strips of lead held the glass in place. The hinged sashes opened outward like doors.

The Big House had no bathroom, of course, and there was no kitchen in it. Mazie, the cook, did her work in a small building next door and Young Tim carried food to the family in the hall. A lot of other small buildings clustered around the Big House like chicks around a hen. Each one had its own use: a storehouse, a smokehouse, a wash house, a tool house, and several cabins for servants. A building called the Freeman's house also stood nearby. Unmarried men who worked for wages lived in it, and traveling strangers could have a bed there.

*The hall*

The parlor of the Big House was for special company. It had a bed in it for guests. The hall was the family living room and dining room. Its walls were covered with smooth boards put on lengthwise. Nearly all of the furniture in the house came from England on tobacco ships. The hall had no sofas or easy chairs in it, just a stiff armchair for the Master, some benches and stools, a long narrow table, and a chest for linen.

The family bought all their clothes in London, too. Alan wrote to the agent who sold his tobacco for him and described what was wanted. The agent sent it over on the ship. In these early days he even sent clothes and shoes for the slaves. When they went to church or went visiting, Alan and Margaret Shaw wore expensive outfits made of silk and velvet. They seldom fitted very well, because the London tailor had to make them by guess.

Before meals, Young Tim warmed the pewter plates and bowls on the hearth in the hall. The family usually ate with wooden spoons or pewter ones. Pewter is tin with a little copper or lead added to it. A few people had the new two-tined iron forks to eat with. A man who owned one carried it with him. Mazie cut up meat so that it would be easy to eat with a spoon. She served it with corn bread which she baked in an iron pot on the kitchen hearth. The adults drank beer with their meals, sometimes with breakfast. Mazie brewed it in a copper kettle. Sometimes the children had milk.

*Mistress Margaret Shaw*

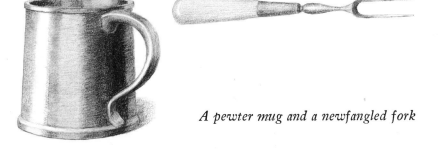

*A pewter mug and a newfangled fork*

The stairs ended in the bedroom over the hall. Whoever used the farther room had to pass through this one first. The Master and Mistress slept in the room at the stairhead, but they didn't sleep alone. Baby Betsy's cradle was on the far side of their bed and Willy, who was three, slept in the low trundle bed on the near side. In the daytime Willy's bed slid under the big one. This big bedstead was much higher than beds are now. Its tall posts held up a wooden frame from which curtains hung. During the day these curtains slid back against the posts, but at night they enclosed the whole bed.

The bed had no springs. The mattress lay on ropes laced from side to side and stretched tight. It was stuffed with goose feathers. So were the pillows. These were large. The Shaws leaned back against them and slept half sitting up. Everyone did this instead of lying flat to sleep as we do. So beds were shorter then than beds are now.

There wasn't much other furniture in the room: two stools, a blanket chest, and a washstand with a pewter basin and a horn comb on it. A very small, very wrinkled, looking glass hung over the washstand. There was no clothes closet; clothes hung on pegs against the wall. There was a warming pan in the room. It was made of copper and it had a lid and a long wooden handle. On chilly nights, Dolly, the maid, put hot coals in it and slid it back and forth between the covers to warm the bed.

The second bedroom had much the same kind of furniture in it. The Shaws' daughters, Flora and Susan, slept there. Six-teen-year-old Wallace, the oldest child, slept in the Freeman's House.

*Dolly, with the warming pan*

*Cutting and spearing tobacco*

Since tobacco was so important, we had better take a look at tobacco "making." That is what the Shaws called the growing and curing of the plant.

Early in the spring Alan Shaw sprouted tobacco seed in special beds and then had the seedlings moved to the fields. The slaves set out the plants in rows, quite far apart, because tobacco plants grow large. Men with hoes kept all the weeds out of the fields. By the end of July, the plants were nearly six feet tall. The slaves then pinched off all of the pink blossoms. This made the big leaves grow still bigger.

About the end of August, workers with big knives cut all the plants off, close to the ground. They thrust a slender stick through the thick stems, close to the cut ends, until they could get no more plants on the stick. A cart hauled loads of the filled sticks to a tobacco barn. There, other men hung them up. They rested the ends of the sticks side by side across beams, so that the green plants hung upside down to cure.

The tobacco barn was like two big log cabins with a wide space between them. One long roof covered the whole thing. The cart drove into the space between the cabins to unload. Gaps between the piled logs let air blow through the barn, but the roof kept rain off the curing tobacco.

After five or six weeks the green leaves dried and turned brown. Then the slaves pulled the leaves off and tied their stems together to make flat bunches that looked like fans. They made piles of the bunches that had only the best leaves in them, and other piles of not-so-good leaves. These lay all winter in the barn while the slaves made big wooden hogsheads to pack them in. In the spring the hogsheads were filled. The men used a long lever to squeeze the bunches of tobacco down until each cask had five hundred pounds in it.

*In the tobacco barn*

17

*The public warehouse and a tobacco ship*

All of the oronookos and many large planters, like the Shaws, hauled their tobacco to public warehouses near the water. Here an inspector examined it and weighed it. He gave the grower a receipt for all of his tobacco. The hogsheads were loaded on a ship and taken to England. There was almost no real money in Virginia or Maryland, so the people used tobacco receipts for money. They even paid taxes with tobacco. This was complicated. The price of tobacco rose and fell, so nobody knew how much a receipt was really worth until after the tobacco had been sold in London. This took about six months, because the sailing ships that brought the news were very slow.

All the larger planters had their own agents, called factors, who sold tobacco for them in London. The factor used the money he got from selling the tobacco to pay for all the things the planter ordered. Sometimes the planter ordered more things than the tobacco would buy, but the factor sent them over, anyway. He paid for them out of his own pocket and then paid himself back with the money he got from the next year's tobacco. He didn't mind doing that because he always charged the planter much more for everything than its actual cost.

All of the planter's money stayed in England. He seldom knew how much he really had, but he always managed to *feel* rich. So he went on buying. Some plantations owed money to their factors for many years. The Shaws never did this, even when they had to do without things. That's one reason why their plantation succeeded.

*Packing a hogshead*

*The sloop and the barge*

The Shaws' field slaves and their families lived in cabins scattered over the plantation. Counting them and the house servants, about forty people lived at Shaw's Fortune. It was like a small village. It had to be because there was no village near it. For a long time, Jamestown, in Virginia, and St. Mary's City, in Maryland, were the only towns on the Chesapeake Bay.

Alan Shaw rode over his plantation on horseback nearly every morning. He knew just what was going on, but his overseer, Harry Beckwith, helped him and saw that things got done. Harry had been a bond servant. When he finished his term he stayed on to earn some money and learn as much as he could. Later he owned a plantation himself. Many of the slaves on the place did special jobs. Dick was the blacksmith; Ben was the carpenter; Jolly took care of the cows; Old Tim took care of the horses.

Mistress Margaret taught the women slaves to sew and to cook. They called her Miss Meg, for short. Some of them worked around the house but most of them worked in the fields with the men. When people on the place got sick, Miss Meg dosed them. There was no doctor to call. The Shaws didn't think they did anything wrong by owning slaves, but the slaves thought they did. Nobody ever wanted to be *owned* by somebody else. The Shaws were kind people, but the thought of a slave rebellion frightened them, so they harshly punished any slave who shirked work or disobeyed orders.

Plantations were far apart and no real roads ran between them, just trails through the forest. When the Shaws visited their neighbors, they usually went in a small sailboat or in a "barge" rowed by four slaves. Either way was more comfortable than riding a horse and usually quicker. Neither the Shaws nor any of their neighbors had a carriage at this time.

The family welcomed visitors. They gave food and a bed even to people they had never seen before. This was because there were no inns where strangers could stay. It was also because visitors brought news. There was not yet one newspaper in all of the American colonies.

The children, too, were glad to see visitors. They heard about distant places that they could hardly imagine: about Boston, with its harbor full of ships; about the Dutch people in New Amsterdam; about the blue mountains far to the west of Shaw's Fortune. There was no regular school where the children could learn. Mistress Duckett, over at Broad Creek Plantation, taught her children to read. Mistress Meg Shaw had never learned to read herself, but her children were learning. Giles Watson, one of the bond servants, had been to school in England. He was glad to teach the children their letters. Nobody thought of teaching the slave children to read; but some of them were friends of the children at the Big House and they played together. Little Tim was their favorite. His father was Young Tim who helped in the house. Young Tim's father was Old Tim.

*A class at Shaw's Fortune*

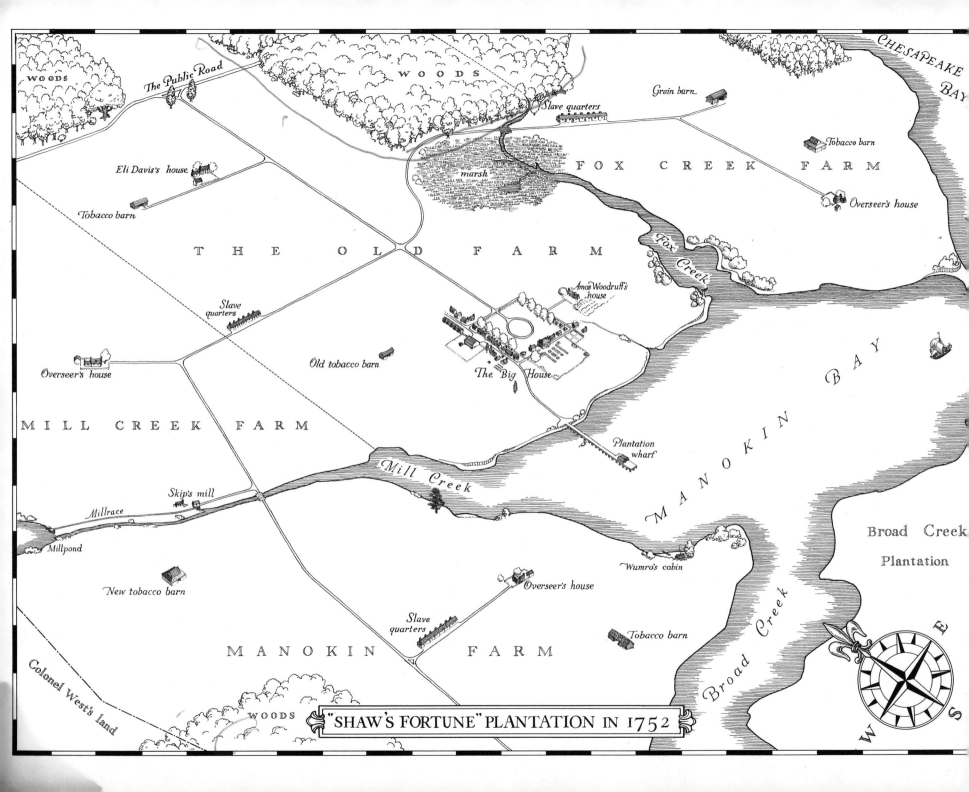

WOODS

The Public Road

WOODS

CHESAPEAKE BAY

Grain barn

Slave quarters

Tobacco barn

Eli Davis's house

marsh

FOX CREEK FARM

Tobacco barn

Overseer's house

THE OLD FARM

Fox Creek

Slave quarters

Amos Woodruff's house

Overseer's house

Old tobacco barn

The Big House

MILL CREEK FARM

MANOKIN BAY

Plantation wharf

Mill Creek

Skip's mill

Broad Creek Plantation

Millrace

Millpond

Wumro's cabin

New tobacco barn

Overseer's house

Broad Creek

Slave quarters

MANOKIN FARM

Tobacco barn

Colonel West's land

WOODS

"SHAW'S FORTUNE" PLANTATION IN 1752

N E S W

This is where we jump forward about a hundred years to 1752. Up in Philadelphia that year Benjamin Franklin is flying his kite to find out if lightning is electricity. (It is.) Shaw's Fortune is now a much bigger place. The Shaws have added three adjoining plantations to their land. Each of these farms has a name and each one has its own overseer. Alan Shaw's original place is now called the Old Farm. The others are Fox Creek Farm, Mill Creek Farm, and Manokin Farm. There are nearly two hundred slaves at Shaw's Fortune now.

Of course, after all this time none of the original people are alive. These Shaws are descendants of Alan and Margaret. The master now is Malcolm Shaw. He is forty-three years old. His wife's name is Sarah but nobody, not even her husband, ever calls her anything but Miss Sally. They have four children. The oldest, Elizabeth, called Betsy, is married to Peter Culp, who manages his father's plantation about twenty miles away. Tom, the Shaws' only son, is fourteen. His sister Ellen is two years younger and Lucy, the youngest, is five. Malcolm Shaw's father, Squire Duncan Shaw, is seventy. He has retired but he lives with the family. Duncan's grandfather was Willy, whom we left sleeping in the trundle bed long ago.

As the years passed the family became important in the colony. All of the plantation masters have been members of the Assembly, which is something like a legislature. Malcolm now belongs to it. Squire Duncan is on the Governor's Council, a kind of senate and court, combined.

Everybody in the family, except Lucy, can read now. When Duncan was twenty he sailed to England on a tobacco ship, and studied at Cambridge University. Malcolm stayed in America and went to William and Mary College in Virginia.

As we look at Shaw's Fortune in 1753, we shall find that some things are much the same but some are very different.

23

THE SHAW FAMILY
IN THEIR
EVERYDAY CLOTHES

Malcolm Shaw

Miss Sally Shaw

Squire Duncan Shaw

Thomas

Lucy

Ellen

*The Big House that Squire Duncan built*

The Shaws have a fine new house. It is called the Big House, just as the old one was, and this one is really big. It has twelve rooms in it. Squire Duncan built it about twenty years ago. He wanted a lot more room, so he kept the old house, too. It is used as space for extra guests. He fixed it up a little and built the new one alongside it with a space between them. At the other end of the new house he built a large outside kitchen.

The new house is more than twice as long as the old one. It is higher, too, because the ceilings of its rooms are higher. Duncan put four of its bedrooms inside the roof and built dormer windows in the roof to give them light.

The style of building has changed since the time of Alan. Duncan used a book, from London, to see how to build but he didn't follow the book exactly. He had some ideas of his own. His house has more windows and bigger ones than Alan's had. The panes of the windows are larger, too, and the wooden sashes slide up and down in their frames, just as ours usually do. White paint on the window and door frames and on the cornice below the roof contrasts with the brick walls and gives the building a bright, cheerful look. The solid shutters are painted dark green. They are not often closed, because slatted venetian blinds inside the windows keep out the hot sun without darkening the rooms.

There is a level lawn in front of the Big House. The gardeners cut its grass with long-bladed scythes, but it never looks as smooth as our lawns look. It will be a hundred years until Mr. Caldwell invents the lawnmower. Sometimes Zenas, the shepherd, lets his sheep graze on the lawn for a few days. They make the grass short. A wide path of flat stones crosses part of the lawn from the doorsteps to the driveway.

The back of this house is almost like its front. It overlooks Manokin Bay, beyond the flower garden and the long slope of the regular sheep pasture.

*Hot food from the kitchen*

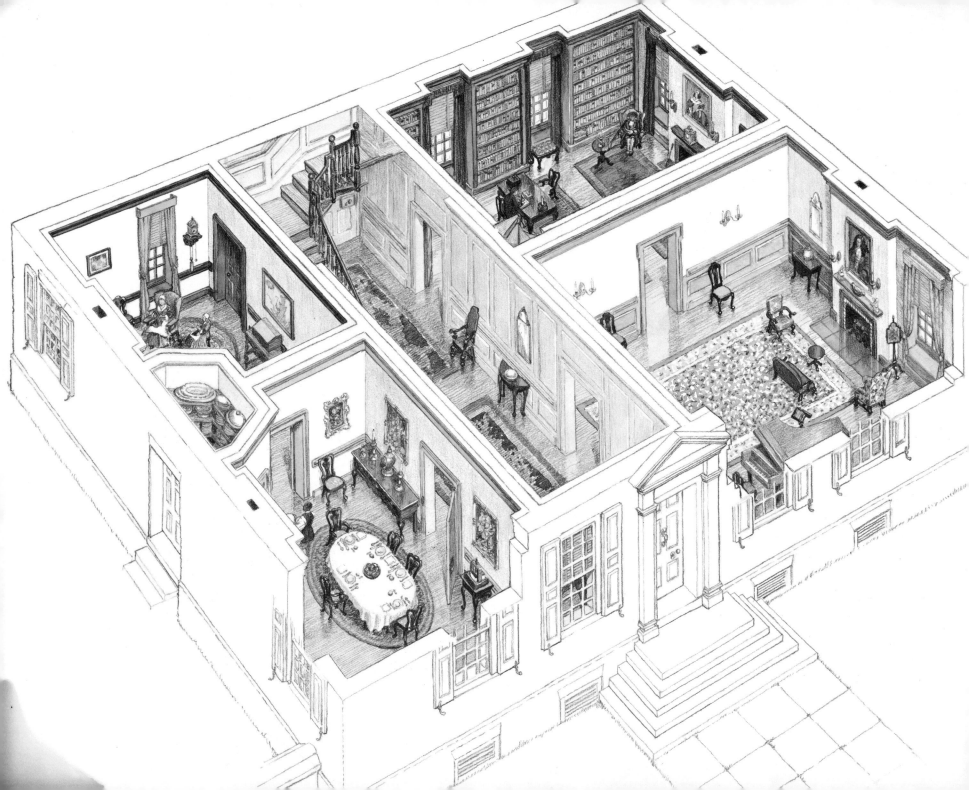

Here is a look inside the first floor of the new house. In the drawing on the opposite page, the top part of the house has been lifted off. Part of the front wall is taken away, too, so that you can see in better. Walk up the wide steps to the front door. It lets you into the stair hall. This is a very cold place in winter because it has no fireplace in it as the other rooms have. The hall runs all the way through the house to the back door. When both doors are open in the summertime, they let a fine breeze blow through. But they also let flies in. This house has no screens anywhere. The hall is pretty dark. It has only one window next to the front door. The stairs go part way up in one flight, then they turn at a landing to get the rest of the way up. The whole hall is paneled with wood painted a deep cream color. Not far from Shaw's Fortune lives Colonel West. He had an English bond servant who was clever at woodwork. Squire Duncan "rented" him from the colonel for months.

You will notice that though the front door is in the middle of the house, the hall is not. This makes the two rooms on the left of the hall smaller than the two on its right, but they are still large rooms. The back room on the left is the sitting room. This is where the family gathers before supper and where Miss Sally sits to sew whenever she has a few free minutes. The front room on this side is the dining room. A door alongside the dining room fireplace leads to a pantry where Pompey, the butler, keeps the silver and the new cream-colored queens-ware dishes. There is some pewter there, too, but it is now used only for breakfast. When Pompey sets the table, he puts on bone-handled steel knives and silver forks for everybody. The knives would seem large to you and the forks very small. The forks have only three tines. A door from the pantry leads to a brick path outside. The kitchen maids use this when they bring

food to the house. In cold weather they run along the path, and Pompey puts the dishes on the hearth in front of the dining room fire to keep warm, just as Young Tim used to do.

*The parlor*

Across the hall from the sitting room is the library. Squire Duncan spends a lot of time here with his books. He has one of the largest collections of books in the colony. Many of them are in Latin. It was he who gave most of the slaves Latin and Greek names. This was a quite usual thing to do. A door beside the library fireplace leads outdoors. This is much used by Malcolm Shaw who works in the room with his secretary, Oliver Bennett. Mr. Shaw writes letters and Oliver copies them all in a large blank book so that they can be kept as well as sent. They both write with sharpened goose quills and blot the ink by shaking sand over it. Together they work on the plantation accounts and make long lists of articles to be ordered from the factor in London. This is one of the things that has not changed. In bad weather, the plantation manager, Eli Davis, comes to the library to talk over his problems with the Master.

Except when they have company, the Shaws seldom use the parlor, at the front of the house. It is a beautiful room, especially when thirty candles are lighted in it at night. These burn in brackets on the wall and in a shiny brass chandelier that hangs from the ceiling. Their light gleams on the polished floor and on the dark walnut furniture. No more benches and stools here; there are chairs for everybody now. A beautiful rug covers the middle of the floor. Its whole surface is embroidered by hand with colored wools in the cross-stitch that is called needle point. Miss Sally Shaw's mother made it, with a lot of help from her slaves, and gave it to her daughter as a wedding present. It is the only thing in the room that was not bought in England. Yellow silk curtains hang at the parlor windows. The windows' sills are so low and so wide that people sit on them.

Miss Sally's harpsichord stands in a corner. She brought it with her when she came to Shaw's Fortune. She plays it quite nicely. It looks like a long, narrow grand piano. But instead of the felt hammers which strike a piano's strings, the harpsichord has stiff quills which pluck the strings when the keys are pressed. The sound is thinner and it twangs a little. Miss Sally is teaching her daughter Ellen to play.

*Lucy and the Squire. Lucy has long "hanging sleeves" attached to her dress. When she was learning to walk, her nurse held her up with them. Lucy hates them now but she will have to go on wearing them until she is six.*

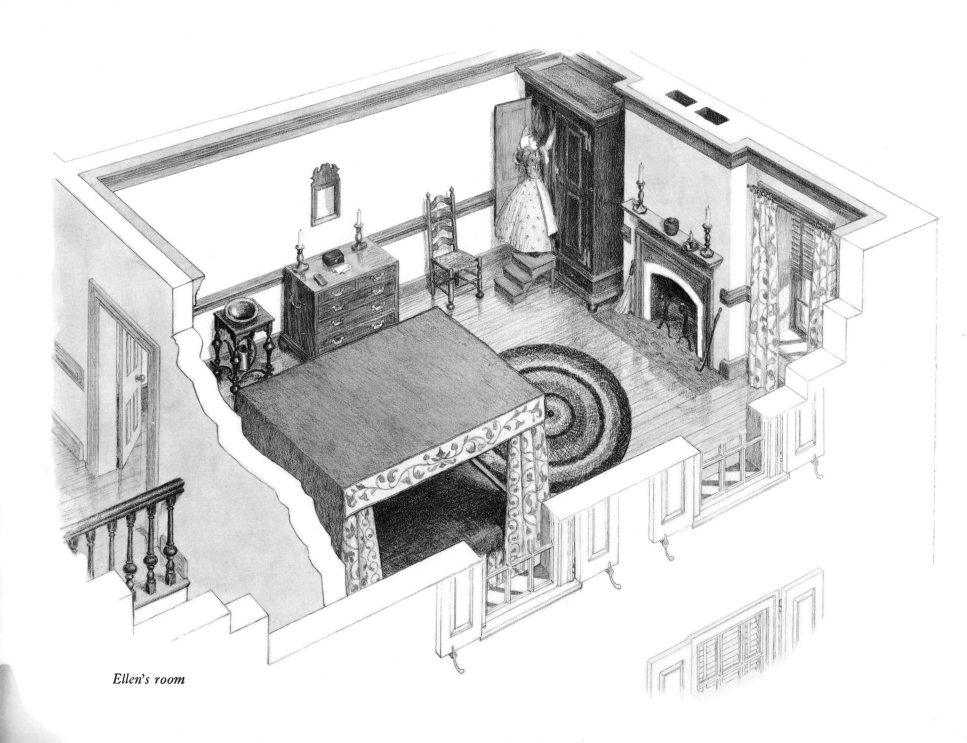

*Ellen's room*

The four rooms on the second floor of the Shaws' house are arranged just like those on the first floor. Squire Duncan's bedroom is over the library. Master Malcolm and Mistress Sally have the large front room on that side, the one over the parlor. The front room across the hall from them is for guests, but little Lucy and her nurse, Thalia, sleep there usually. Thalia's little girl, Hebe, is Lucy's playmate. Tom has one of the four smaller rooms on the third floor. But there are no fireplaces up there, so he doesn't stay in it long in the winter.

Ellen sleeps in the room over the sitting room. Her room might seem a little bare to you but she thinks it's pretty. There are no pictures on its walls; only one small looking glass that she is very proud of. The walls and ceiling are plain white plaster. The window curtains and the curtains of the high four-poster bed are white linen, and they have flowers and birds embroidered on them with colored wool.

A chest of drawers stands against one wall. Ellen keeps some of her clothes in it. The looking glass hangs over the chest. On one side of the chest is a washstand, looking like a square table with a shelf under it. On the other side is the only chair, very stiff and straight. Ellen's wardrobe, where she keeps most of her clothes, stands in the corner by the fireplace. It is so high that Ellen can't reach the pegs the clothes hang on. So Cato, the carpenter, built her a wooden step to stand on. She has another like it that she uses for climbing in and out of bed.

On cool mornings, before Ellen is awake, the housemaid, Clio, comes into the room. She carries a pan with a few hot coals in it. She puts one of them under some kindling wood in the fireplace and blows on it to start the fire. She can't use a match because matches haven't been invented yet. As Clio goes out she wakes Ellen, but Ellen stays under the covers until the room warms up.

*There are three Ellens here. Ellen is getting ready for a dancing party. Though she is only twelve, she goes to grown-up parties, and so does her brother, Tom. At the left, wearing her linen shift and her stays, Ellen tries on the new farthingale which will hold her dress out at the sides. She can collapse it to get through narrow doors. Next, she is all decked out in her new sack dress, with her hair up and her lace mitts on. "La!" says Ellen, "Am I not a grand lady?" Last, she's ready to go, snug in a hooded pelisse, with her fan in her muff. Below are one of her mitts and one of her dancing shoes.*

Field work at Shaw's Fortune starts at sunrise—half past four in midsummer. The top edge of the sun just shows on this July morning as Malcolm Shaw and Tom step out of the kitchen. They have stopped there for a snack, bread and milk for the boy, beer and cold ham for the man. They both wear linen breeches and canvas "spatterdashes," which are leggings. Their white shirts are open at the neck for this hot weather. Both of them have on wide-brimmed straw hats. They mount the horses that are waiting for them and start the daily round of the plantation. Tom doesn't have to go, but he never misses it if he can help it. Sometimes Ellen goes, too, but not today. Trump, Tom's big brown dog, runs from somewhere to join the expedition.

Eli Davis meets them in the lane beyond the front lawn. Eli was a boy when he sailed from Boston on a schooner that traded salt fish for pork and tobacco. When the boat left the Shaw's Fortune wharf, Eli stayed behind. Now, nothing is done on the place that he doesn't know about.

The horses amble out the long lane between two fields of tobacco. It stands seven feet high in full leaf and will be ready to cut in two weeks. The three turn left on the lane that leads to the Mill Creek Farm, but almost at once they turn into a field on their right. Flax grew here. Some days ago it was all pulled up by the roots and heaped in piles to "ret." This really means rot. A little rotting doesn't harm the linen fiber but it does make the tough stalks brittle, so that they will break up easily. Field hands are now opening the piles with wooden forks and spreading them to dry in the sun.

The overseer in charge brings a handful of flax to the Master and the manager. They break a stalk or two and see that it is in good shape. Tom tries it too, and asks Mr. Davis questions about it. The flax will be stored in a barn as soon as it is dry. In the fall the men will break the stalks on a heavy flax brake that stands on four legs. This doesn't damage the fiber. Neither does scutching, which they do next to knock most of the stalk out of the fiber. The scutcher holds a bunch of plants across the end of an upright plank and slashes at it with a wooden scutching "knife." Now the flax begins to look like linen but it still has bits of stalk in it.

*Braking*

*Scutching*

33

*Skip's mill*

"I'd like you to look at the new barn," Eli says.

"Very well," says Malcolm, "but let us first stop at the mill; I wish to have a word with Skip."

The three continue along the lane toward Mill Creek. Corn grows high on both sides of them. A tobacco plantation now raises many things besides tobacco. Shaw's Fortune has field after field of corn. It feeds animals and people. The cows and oxen eat the dried leaves as fodder; the horses, the pigs, and the chickens, ducks, and geese eat the grain. The people eat quantities of the grain ground up as corn meal.

Just before they reach the bridge over Mill Creek, the riders turn upstream to Skip's mill. His name is really Scipio, but nobody ever calls him that. Almost at once they hear the splash of water turning the mill wheel and the rumble of the grinding millstones. Two men are hoisting sacks of shelled corn from an ox cart up to a small door on the second floor of the mill. "Shelled" means grains taken off the cob. Children and old people shell the corn by scraping the ears against the edge of a pail. These sacks come from Colonel West's plantation. He has no mill, so Skip grinds his corn and takes a little of the meal as "toll" to pay for the grinding.

The new arrivals tie their horses and go into the mill. Inside, the noise of the stones is so loud that you can't hear a man

*Corn*

shout. When Skip sees them, he pulls a handle and shuts off the water. The noise dies away as the mill wheel stops turning.

"Good morning, Skip. How are the new stones?"

"Mornin', suh. They *good* ones!"

"That is excellent! You and Tote did well to get them in so quickly."

Behind the bins stands a thick wooden shaft. It is turned, below the floor, by the water wheel. Above the ceiling, the shaft's upper end turns the upper millstone. The lower stone stands still; the shaft passes through it without moving it. When Tom climbs the steep stair to the second floor and looks through the dusty little window, he can just glimpse the dam and the millpond far upstream. A wide ditch brings water from the pond to the mill. This water pours onto the top of the water wheel and floods the downstream face of its rim. The rim is quite wide and it has small troughs across it which fill with water. As they pass under the bottom of the wheel they empty themselves. The "wet" side of the wheel is always heavier than its "dry" side, so the wheel keeps turning.

Inside, on the second floor, Tom sees little more than sacks of grain and a large box with a square funnel over it. The two millstones lie flat inside the box, one on the other. The funnel is called the hopper. Skip empties the sacks of corn into it. The corn runs from the bottom of the hopper into a hole made in the middle of the upper millstone. This stone grinds it against the lower stone. Ground meal falls from the edges of the stones into the box. From there it slides down a chute into a bin. Skip's helper, Tote, scoops meal from this bin and sifts it into another one to get the coarse parts out of it. The bottom of his round sifter is covered with stretched sheepskin. Hundreds of small holes, burned through the skin with a hot wire, let only the fine meal fall through.

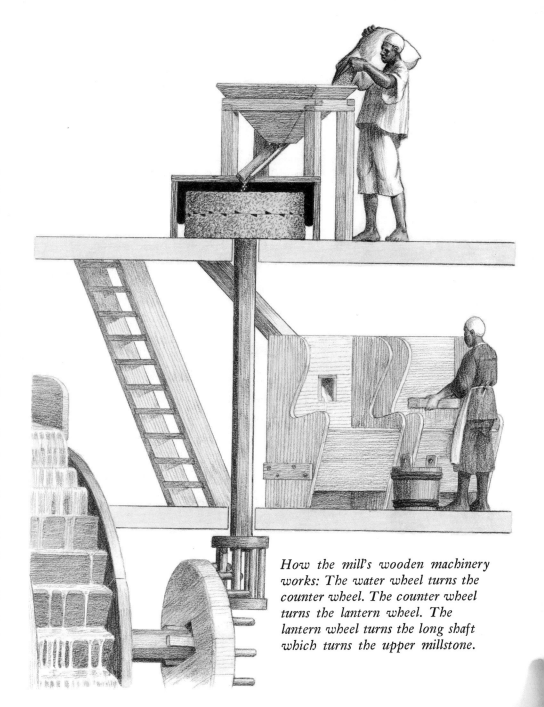

*How the mill's wooden machinery works: The water wheel turns the counter wheel. The counter wheel turns the lantern wheel. The lantern wheel turns the long shaft which turns the upper millstone.*

*The new tobacco barn*

*Splitting shingles*

*Shaving shingles*

*A frow for splitting*

*A drawknife for shaving*

Tom and his father and Eli have crossed the bridge over Mill Creek and are riding up a low hill on Manokin Farm. They hear the sounds of sawing, chopping, and hammering. The new tobacco barn stands on top of the hill, surrounded by more growing tobacco. It isn't finished, but work on it is well along. This is a different kind of building from the log one that Alan Shaw used. Even its shape is different. It looks like a house with a wide shed all the way around it.

Most of the roof is finished, but two men are still nailing shingles in rows on the high part of the roof. Down below, two men are making shingles for the roofers. One splits thin boards from a block of wood about as long as your arm. The second man uses a two-handled drawknife to shave the shingles thin on one end. This is so the next row of shingles will lie flat when it is nailed over the tapered ends. The man with the drawknife straddles a bench and uses his foot to press a lever. This causes a clamp to grip the thick end of the shingle while he shaves it. He calls his bench a "shingle horse."

Another pair of men are nailing up-and-down boards to the side of the barn. They nail half of the boards at both ends but every other board they leave loose at the bottom. When tobacco is curing in the barn, these loose boards will be propped open in dry weather, but propped shut when it rains.

Two other workers make boards for the nailers. They saw them lengthwise from a squared timber which lies across two high trestles. The "top sawyer" stands on the timber and guides the long saw. He also pulls the saw up after his partner, the "pitman," pulls it down. The pitman works in a shower of sawdust. His down-pull is the one that does the cutting, so he works harder than the top sawyer does. If these men should cut each plank clear off, the timber would soon get too narrow for the top sawyer to stand on. So they stop each cut a little short and leave all the planks fastened together at the far end.

Nearby, an axman is squaring a new timber for the sawyers. He starts with a round log and chops away bark and wood from one side at a time. He uses a special broadax which has a very wide blade and a short, crooked handle. As soon as he gets one side flat, he turns the log to lie on it. Before he starts a new cut he snaps a chalk line along the log to make a guide. To do this he first covers a string with chalk dust. Then he gets two people, one at each end, to stretch the string tight along the bark. When he lifts the string and lets it go, it snaps down and marks the log from end to end with a perfectly straight line.

While Malcolm Shaw and Eli talk to Cato, who is in charge of the work, Tom goes into the barn. The new wood in there smells good. Thick posts, each twice as high as the ceiling of your room, hold up the corners of the main roof. A lot more posts, only one ceiling high, support the outer edges of the shed roof. Squared cross timbers connect the posts. The ends of these are locked into the posts and are held in place by wooden pins. The pins are treenails but Cato calls them "trunnels." They are driven into holes bored clear through the posts and the cross timbers.

"She seems to be comin' on, Cato," says Eli Davis, "but don't slow up. We're goin' to start cuttin' t'bacca week after next."

"She be ready, suh," says Cato.

*Sawing planks*

*Hewing timber*

*A broadax*

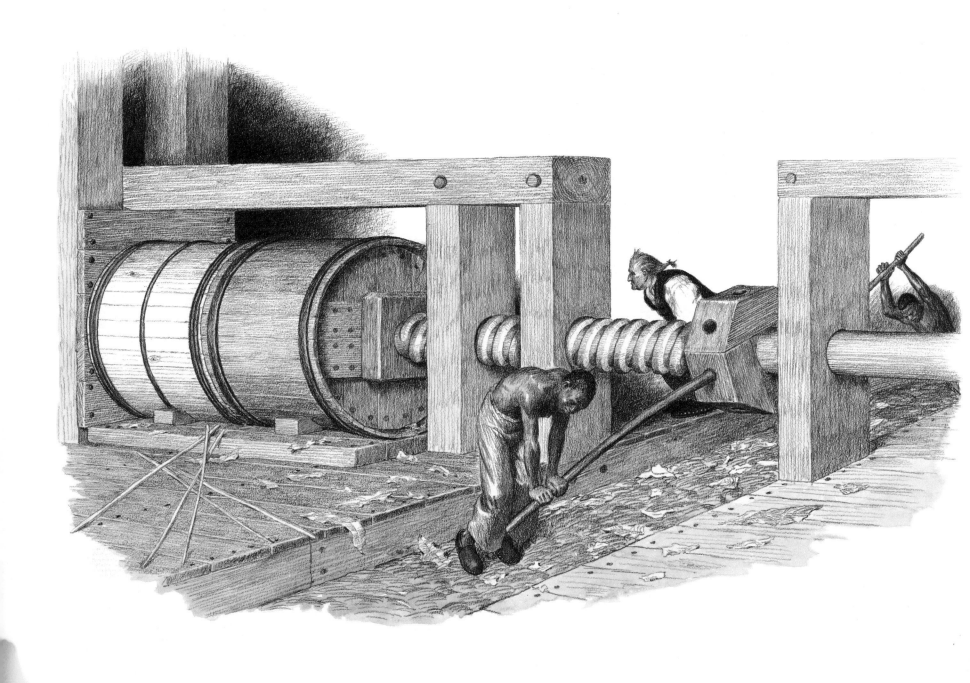

When the barn is finished, the big "tobacco prize" will be moved from the Old Farm and put into it. The prize is a press which squeezes tobacco into hogsheads for shipping. It can get a lot more into one hogshead than Alan Shaw's old lever could.

The slaves make the hogsheads. They are like large barrels, except their sides don't bulge as a barrel's sides do. Stood on end, a hogshead is as tall as an eight-year-old boy. He could walk right into one turned on its side. The body of a hogshead is made of rather thin wooden slats. The slaves stand these in a circle and tie a rope around them to hold them together while they nail the hoops on. The hoops are split saplings. A hogshead gets five of them: two around each end and one around the middle. Circular heads, made of slats, go in each end. One is put in before the the hogshead is filled and the other afterward.

A hogshead to be "prized" is first stuffed with as much tobacco as can be put in it by hand. Then it is laid on its side in the press and another hogshead, called the cask, is placed in front of its open end. The cask has no ends. It, too, is stuffed with tobacco. The men turn the wooden screw of the press. This moves it forward and it slowly pushes the tobacco out of the cask and into the hogshead, on top of what is already there.

The slaves use the sticks that the leaves were cured on to hold the tobacco in the hogshead while they back the screw out and fill up the cask again. Then they pull the sticks and work hard to squeeze one more load into the hogshead. They nail in the head to keep it there.

The hogsheads are stored in the barn until the time comes to load them on the ship. But nobody can tell just when the ship will get here. Shaw's Fortune now "makes" so much tobacco that it has its own wharf. Oxcarts will take the hogsheads down there.

*Making a hogshead*

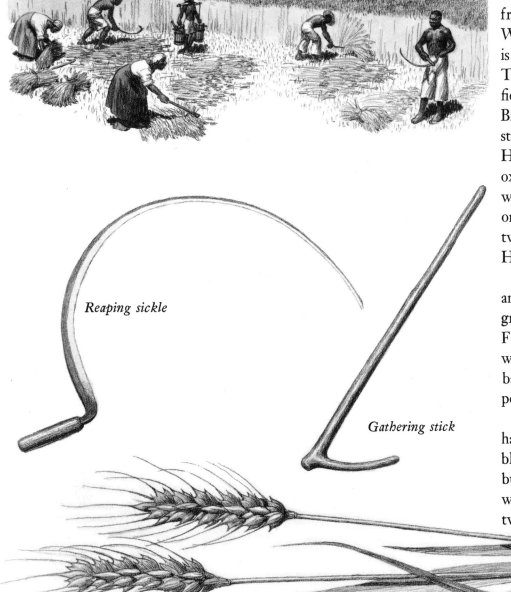

*Reaping sickle*

*Gathering stick*

*Wheat*

As they leave the barn, the horsemen can see most of Shaw's Fortune, a patchwork of fields and woods. Broad Creek lies on their right, the Big House a little to their left, and in front of them, Manokin Bay, silver in the morning sunlight. Wumro, the old Indian who lives as he pleases on the place, is out there fishing for his breakfast from his dugout canoe. The riders return as they came: across the bridge, past the flax field, and then on beyond the lane that brought them from the Big House. Their way takes them through the woods that stands partly on the Old Farm and partly on Fox Creek Farm. Here they say good morning to Cicero, who is loading his oxcart from a woodpile that was cut last winter. "Sis" hauls wood from one year's end to the next. In summer he needs only this small cart to feed all the cooking fires. In winter, two large carts are needed to keep fires burning in the Big House and in all the cabins.

Beyond the woods the horses pass more fields with tobacco and corn in them and fields with stubble where oats and barley grew. Beyond these, covering more than half of Fox Creek Farm, stand fields of ripe wheat. The bearded heads are heavy with grain. Most of this wheat will be shipped to England in barrels, but Skip grinds some of it into coarse flour for the people on the plantation.

Twenty men are now harvesting the wheat with sickles. These have narrow blades that are twice as long as modern sickle blades. A woman follows each man and gathers the straw into bundles, called sheaves. She uses a hooked stick to pull the wheat toward her. When she has gathered a sheaf, she quickly twists a handful of straw into a kind of rope and ties it around the bundle. The women leave the sheaves on the ground. Two men pick them up with wooden forks and toss them up to a third man who stands in a cart. He catches the sheaves and places them carefully on the load. When the cart is piled high, it starts for a nearby barn. The loading crew gets a quick drink from the water boy and then moves to an empty cart.

Malcolm and Eli chat with the overseer and examine the wheat to see that it is properly dry, then they move on to the barn. Men are stowing wheat in both ends of the building, leaving a clear space through the middle for threshing. The carts bring the wheat into this space through one door and leave, empty, through the opposite one.

The threshers will spread the straw on the floor. They will then beat it with flails. A flail has a long handle with a club attached to it, end-to-end, by a loose leather thong. Holding the handle, the thresher swings the club over his head and brings it down on the straw with a thump. It takes many thumps to knock the kernels out of their husks and onto the floor under the straw.

The men rake the straw up and stow it in the barn. Then they sweep up the grain and winnow it. This gets out the chaff, which is the beards, empty husks, and bits of broken straw. They lift the grain in baskets up to a man on a platform, and he pours it from there onto the floor again. The breeze that moves through the barn blows the chaff out. If there is no breeze, the men make one with big square fans.

"Tom," says Malcolm, "I think it's time for breakfast."

"Yes, sir," says Tom, who has been thinking that for some time.

*Wooden pitchfork*

*Threshing*

41

Tom has washed his hands and face at the well and put on a neckcloth and a light coat that he keeps hanging in the back of the hall under the stairs. The neckcloth is a white band about as wide as your wrist. It goes twice around Tom's neck and hangs down in front. Tom is in the dining room before Pompey finishes ringing the breakfast bell. Malcolm and Miss Sally and Ellen come in from the sitting room. It is ten o'clock, the usual breakfast time at Shaw's Fortune. Dinner is at four in the afternoon; supper is at nine in the evening. "Evening" is the whole time between dinner and supper.

Malcolm has put on a tan linen suit and a plain brown wig. The ends of the black scarf around his neck hang down to his waist. Duncan Shaw comes from the library wearing a flowered dressing gown, known as a "banyan" and a silk "turban" in place of his wig. These men always cover their heads when they are not wearing wigs, because their own hair is shaved off.

Miss Sally's white cap covers her hair except for a few brown curls in front. Her dress is cotton, printed all over with small red flowers. She bought the cloth in England, but it was made in India. The dress has a tight bodice and tight sleeves with large cuffs at the elbows. Miss Sally wears a white neckerchief. Her skirt is open in the front and is caught up in back so that it drapes on the sides. This shows most of her light blue underskirt. She has on a short white apron; she almost always does.

Ellen's pink-and-white striped dress is much like her mother's, but her cuffs are smaller and her skirt hangs to her ankles all the way around. She, too, wears an apron. Her blonde hair hangs loose below her cap. Miss Sally's shoes are buckled, but Tom and Ellen tie their everyday shoes with short strings, called latchets.

When company comes, Pompey serves dinner wearing a white wig and a blue coat with a lot of gold braid on it. The coat has flaring skirts, and cuffs so big that they reach to his elbows. Pompey is proud of that coat. But this morning he is bareheaded, and a long plum-colored vest, buttoned over his fat stomach, reaches halfway to his knees. His shirt sleeves are very full. His knee breeches are dull yellow, his stockings white, and his black shoes are fastened with polished pewter buckles.

Though the Shaws have fruit on the table for other meals, they do not eat it for breakfast; and they have never heard of tomato juice. They call tomatoes "love apples" and think that they are poisonous. This morning Pompey passes a plate of sliced cold ham, a big round pewter charger piled with small fried fish, and a covered bowl filled with hot "corndodgers." These are thick corn meal pancakes. Tom puts molasses on his and puts away five of them. Everybody has tea. They stir milk and sugar into it and then pour it out of the cup and drink it from the saucer.

Breakfast is a time for planning the day. Malcolm says he is going to ride over to Colonel West's to talk to him about repairing the church roof. At once Tom and Ellen want to go along, but they are told that Mr. Bennett is waiting for them at the schoolhouse. They expected this, so they excuse themselves and leave.

Miss Sally says, "Don't forget, the Osborns are coming for dinner."

"Then I must be shaved," Malcolm says, "Pomp, send Caesar up to shave me in about half an hour." Caesar works in the house, helping Pompey where he is needed.

"Caesar has a new son. I'm going to call on him as soon as I've seen Mandy about dinner," says Miss Sally, as she picks up her straw hat and goes out.

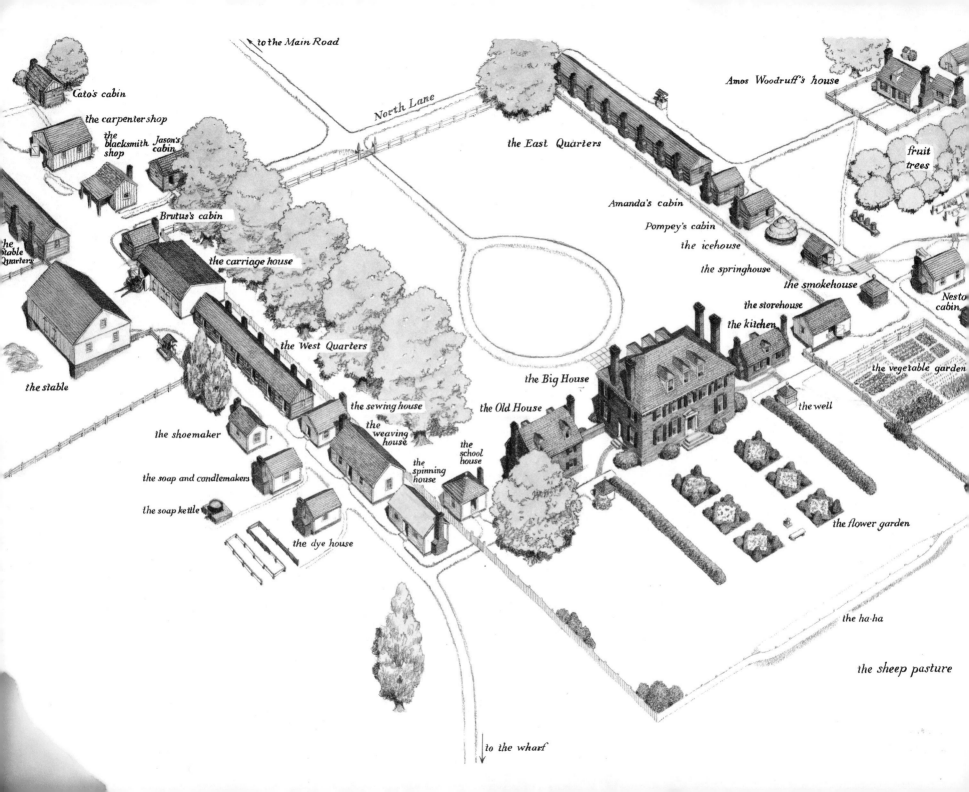

to the Main Road

North Lane

Amos Woodruff's house

Cato's cabin

the carpenter shop

the blacksmith shop

Jason's cabin

the East Quarters

fruit trees

Brutus's cabin

the stable Quarters

the carriage house

Amanda's cabin

Pompey's cabin

the icehouse

the springhouse

the smokehouse

Nesto cabin

the West Quarters

the storehouse

the kitchen

the stable

the vegetable garden

the well

the sewing house

the Old House

the Big House

the shoemaker

the weaving house

the school house

the soap and candlemakers

the spinning house

the flower garden

the soap kettle

the dye house

the ha-ha

the sheep pasture

to the wharf

Before we lose track of Miss Sally, let's take a look at where she is likely to go. Malcolm Shaw runs the plantation, but his wife takes care of the people on the place. She is busy at it all day and she starts almost as early in the morning as her husband does.

You remember the small buildings that clustered around Alan Shaw's house? There are many more of these now; they extend around three sides of the lawn. Shaw's Fortune is still like a village. Each building has a label in the "helicopter view" on the opposite page. In the next few pages you will find out what goes on in them.

The buildings on the kitchen side and along the East Lane all serve the Big House. Pompey and Amanda, as head servants, have their separate cabins where they live with their families. The rest of the house servants live in the quarters. These are cabins, too, but they are joined together in a row, like a motel. Across the lawn, along the West Lane, are the workshops where clothes are made for the slaves. Slaves also make the clothes. Miss Sally watches over their work and Carrie Woodruff shows them how to do it. Amos Woodruff is the overseer of the Old Farm and Carrie is his wife.

The quarters on the West Lane are for the gardeners and for the women who work in the shops. Next to them is the carriage house and facing that, across the stable yard, is the stable for the family horses. The West Lane runs right through the stable yard. Brutus, the coachman, has charge of all the carriages and the twelve horses. His cabin is beyond the carriage house.

Just beyond the North Lane is the shop and cabin of the big blacksmith, Jason. There is a shed on the front of the shop. Here the horses stand while Jason puts new shoes on their hoofs. Jason is an easy man; the horses like him. They stand quietly on three legs while he lifts a hoof and nails an iron shoe on it. He never hurts them when he does this.

Next to the blacksmith shop is Cato's carpenter shop. He and some of his helpers work there in bad weather when nothing can be done outside. Sometimes they build wheelbarrows and carts. When they do, Jason make the iron parts for them.

Just back of the Big House is the flower garden. Nearby, on the kitchen side, is the vegetable garden. Here Nestor, the head gardener, grows cabbages, turnips, beets, parsnips, beans, squashes, and sweet corn, though no potatoes or tomatoes. He does have asparagus, melons, and strawberries. Nestor and his helpers also take care of the flower garden. But Miss Sally tells them what to plant there and where to plant it. The garden's diamond-shaped beds have paths between them. Each bed is edged with a low boxwood hedge that Nestor keeps clipped. Some of the beds have roses in them. The flowers of these are smaller than most roses nowadays, but they bloom thickly on quite tall bushes. One of them, called the *York and Lancaster*, has flowers that are part red and part white.

You will notice that the grounds of the Big House have fences around them. These keep the chickens, the ducks, the turkeys, the big gray geese, and the sheep off the lawns. Squire Duncan Shaw didn't want a fence to show below the garden. He liked the view of the water better without it. So he had a deep, wide ditch dug and put the fence out of sight in that. It still keeps the sheep out. A fence hidden like this is called a ha-ha.

When Miss Sally left the breakfast table, she passed through Pompey's pantry and followed the path to the back door of the kitchen. This door is open, so is the front door opposite it, so are the two windows. Flies come in and out—mostly in. The kitchen is as wide as the hall of Alan Shaw's old house and a bit longer. From beyond a partition you can hear the chatter of the maids washing pots in the scullery. A scullery is a room for pot washing. The kitchen floor is brick; its plaster walls are whitewashed; its ceiling is smoked almost black.

The fireplace takes up most of one end wall. It is so wide and so high that Amanda can walk into it. The fire needs only a small space in the middle of the hearth. A ham cooks over it in a big iron pot which hangs from one of the two cranes. These are iron brackets hinged to the back corners of the fireplace. By swinging them, Amanda can move pots over the fire to cook rapidly, or only near enough to simmer. If she just wants to keep a pot warm, she sets it on the hearth alongside the fire.

Amanda's cooking utensils are iron. Her pots have arched handles like buckets, but they also have three legs to stand on. Her frying pans have long legs to let them stand over the fire. They have long handles too, so that she can move them without burning her hands. Her cooking forks and spoons also have long handles.

There is a square iron door up in the wall beside the fireplace. Behind the door there is a brick recess like a small fireplace. In a way it *is* a fireplace. Its little chimney leads into the big one. Amanda builds a fire in it to get it hot. Then she rakes the fire out and puts her loaves of bread in to bake. This is her oven.

As Miss Sally steps into the kitchen, a boy sitting on a low stool is slowly turning the handle of a spit on which a goose roasts in front of the fire. The spit is a thin iron rod a lot longer than the boy. It passes right through the goose and rests across two hooks on the andirons. The goose turns with the spit so that it cooks evenly on all sides. A flat pan on the hearth catches dripping grease. Amanda bastes the goose by dipping grease from the pan with a spoon and pouring it, sizzling, over the carcass.

"Good morning, Mandy. Good morning, Leonidas. That smells delicious!" The boy grins and ducks his head.

"Mornin', Miss Sally," says Amanda.

"I smell goose and ham; what else is for dinner?"

"Well," Amanda counts on her fingers, "Sof' crabs, green corn, little beets, an' green beans. My girl's pickin' blackberries. All right?"

"Fine, Mandy. I think there'll be only three extra for dinner, but you never know who might drop in."

"No ma'am! Might be the army of Pharaoh!"

Miss Sally chuckles and goes out. As she opens the gate at the corner, she sees a light wagon in the lane by the open storehouse door. Carrie Woodruff is inside dealing out corn meal for Old Mose to deliver to the cabins and quarters near the Big House. He will be all the rest of the day at it.

"Where are you going when you finish here, Carrie?"

"To the weaving house, Miss Sally. I have to help young Dorcas. Yesterday was her first time at the loom, you know."

"I'll see you there later."

*The East Quarters*

On the door of the brick smokehouse a padlock as big as a bun protects the hams and bacon hanging inside. As Miss Sally turns the corner into the East Lane she can hear the women in the wash house singing as they work. They wash here every day to keep the Big House supplied with fresh linen.

Moving up the lane, the Mistress pauses a moment to chat with Chloe, one of the kitchen maids, who is churning butter at the door of the springhouse. Inside, milk in deep pans is kept cool in troughs filled with running spring water.

The icehouse is next to the springhouse. It is a deep, round pit lined with bricks and covered with a thatched roof that seems almost to sit on the ground. Thatch lets in less heat than shingles would. The pit is filled with blocks of ice which were taken from the millpond last January. A covering of sawdust makes the ice last all summer. The icehouse is the only place where the Shaws can keep fresh meat from spoiling.

Though Sally Shaw goes to the quarters to see that they are in good order, she also goes to visit. This morning there is a special reason for going. She wants to admire Caesar and Celia's new baby boy. Celia is one of the spinsters.

The cabins of the quarters are built of logs, hewn square like the timbers of the tobacco barn. But here they are piled one on another to make walls. Their ends lap over at the corners. They are cut thinner where they lap, to make them lie close together. The gaps between the logs are filled with plaster to keep cold out.

Like all the others, Caesar's cabin has just one room. The logs show on the inside of it, but they are neatly whitewashed. It has only one door, with a small brick fireplace opposite it. A plain table stands against the wall. In a corner a rough bedstead, with a straw-stuffed mattress on it, is nailed to the walls. There are two crude stools and a bench to sit on. That is all

of the furniture except a brand new cradle in front of the fire. Cato made it as a gift, because Celia is his daughter. Miss Sally has brought presents, too: a small woolen blanket for the baby and a dozen candles for Celia. Celia will need extra light when she gets up at night to tend the baby.

*Caesar's cabin*

49

*Spinning wool*

Miss Sally has now crossed the lawn in front of the Big House and has gone to see the spinsters. A number of women work in the building. Not all of them spin. Three young girls are hatcheling flax to get the last bits of stalk out of it. The hatchels are really combs, but they look like big brushes with iron spikes for bristles. They lie flat with the spikes up and the girls drag the flax through them. They comb the flax with finer and finer hatchels. Canvas and sacking will be made from the coarse "tow" that sticks in the spikes.

Wool also has to be prepared for spinning. Burrs and matted knots must be picked out by hand and the grease washed out with hot water and soap. Two old women in the spinning house are carding wool that has been dyed blue with indigo. Each has two cards. These are square wooden paddles thickly studded on one side with hooked wire teeth. The women put a handful of wool between the cards and drag the teeth through it. Then they fluff the wool into a cigar-shaped "sliver." The sliver is ready to be spun into yarn.

Spinning is simply twisting into a thread; but the spinster needs skill to keep lumps out of the thread as she adds fiber to it. A rotating spike, called the spindle, does the twisting. A

*Carding wool*

spinning wheel turns its spindle very fast. At Shaw's Fortune, little Negro girls turn the large wool wheels. A distaff, under the spinster's left arm, holds slivers of wool wrapped loosely on it. As the spindle twists one end of the yarn, the spinster holds the other end and adds slivers to it. She moves straight back from the end of the spindle as her yarn gets longer. When she has spun several yards, she moves sideways and lets the yarn wind up on the spindle. She spins and winds until the spindle is full. Then she unwinds the wool by hand onto a reel.

The spinning wheel for flax is small. The spinster sits down to work and turns her own wheel with one foot on a treadle. Her spindle has a hollow end. The yarn goes into it as it twists and comes out again through a hole in the side of the spindle. A simple gadget winds the yarn on a spool. The spool holds a lot, so a flax spinster can make a long yarn without stopping.

Eight women spin flax here and four spin wool. It takes four spinners to make enough yarn for one weaver; three weavers work at Shaw's Fortune. They need more flax than wool because the slaves wear linen in summer and their winter clothes are linsey-woolsey, which is linen and wool mixed.

*Spinning flax*

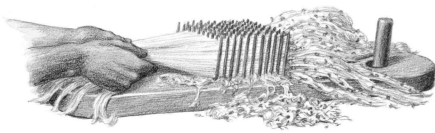

*Hatcheling flax*

51

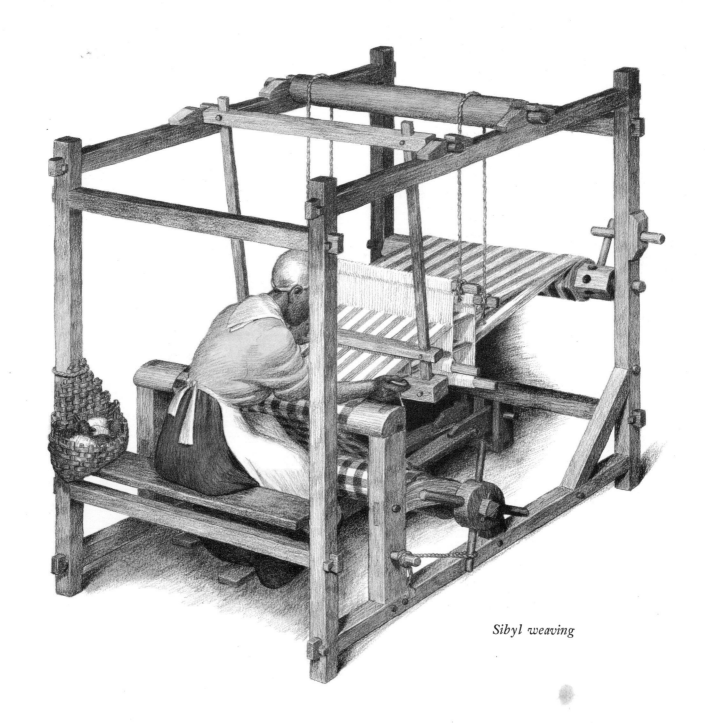

*Sibyl weaving*

Miss Sally finds Carrie Woodruff in the weaving house beside young Dorcas's loom. It is as big as Ellen's bed and is much the same shape. It is built of squared timbers, like a barn. Dorcas's bench is so high that her feet don't touch the floor. She sits on it now, stiff with uncertainty. She and Sibyl are both weaving linsey-woolsey; Daphne weaves linen. Daphne's loom and Sibyl's both sound a steady *thump—thump —thump—thump*. Dorcas's goes *thump——thump———thump-THUMP*.

Let's look at Sibyl's loom and not disturb Dorcas. Hundreds of linen yarns lie side by side to make a strip as wide as a card table that stretches from the back of the loom to a rounded beam just above Sibyl's knees. These yarns are called warps. Sibyl's feet rest on two narrow treadles. When she presses a treadle, she "opens" the warps; half of them (every other one) move upward and the other half move downward. Sibyl throws her shuttle so that it slides across, through the opening. She catches it on the other side. Next she pulls the batten forward and makes that thump we heard. Then she presses the other treadle. The up warps move down and the down warps move up. She throws the shuttle back and catches it again.

What has happened? Look at the shuttle. It is shaped like a boat and is about as long as a man's foot. Its polished wood lets it slide easily across the warps. It is hollow, and a reel inside it is wound with wool yarn. The slightest pull turns the reel and lets the yarn run out through a hole in the shuttle. So, when Sibyl throws her shuttle through the warp, it leaves a strand of yarn behind it. This strand is a weft. When she presses a treadle the warps cross around the weft and hold it.

What about the batten? Sibyl thumps it against each new weft to pack the yarn in place. The two crossbars of the batten, one above the warp and one below, hold a kind of comb between them. This is called the reed. One warp yarn passes through each of the spaces between its teeth. The batten can move forward and back without disturbing the warps.

As Sibyl weaves, the new cloth grows away from her toward the reed. When it gets too close, she doesn't have room enough for the shuttle. She then gets off her bench and rolls the cloth forward on a roller. The warps move forward with it.

Miss Sally pats Dorcas's shoulder. "You'll get it, my dear. Don't try to hurry. It's like a dance. Right foot, right hand, *thump!* Left foot, left hand, *thump!* I know you can dance; I've seen you do it. Make up a little song to go with it."

"Yes'm," says Dorcas in a little voice.

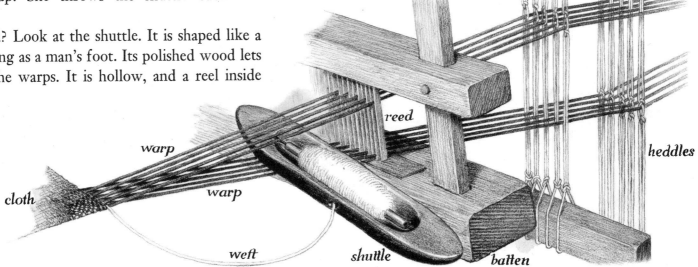

cloth

warp

warp

weft

shuttle

reed

heddles

batten

*Making shoes*

*Dipping candles*

The inside of the sewing house is a square room with four windows and a fireplace. Shelves on both sides of the door hold rolls of blue cloth. At a long table near one wall, Diana, the head seamstress, is cutting linsey-woolsey with big shears. Her daughter helps her by holding the cloth and by gathering up scraps that can be used to patch old clothes.

Across the room four women sit in a group stitching garments. They do all of their sewing by hand; nobody has ever seen a sewing machine. Their thread and their needles came from England. Only an expert can spin linen tight enough for thread. The seamstresses are making winter clothes of linsey-woolsey for the slaves. Next winter they will make summer clothes. These have the same shapes as winter ones but they are made of blue linen. Diana and her helpers also make stockings out of pieces of cloth seamed together.

The men wear short smocks and loose floppy pants. The women wear close-fitting blouses, and full skirts down to their ankles. Children who are older than toddlers wear these same things, but smaller of course.

Across the lane from the sewing house two men make shoes.

The shoes of a pair made at Shaw's Fortune are exactly alike, not lefts and rights, and either shoe can be worn on either foot. They aren't pretty or comfortable but they are strong. The shoemakers sew the uppers onto the soles with strong linen thread. They use sharp awls to make holes in the leather for each stitch. Men's work shoes have an extra sole nailed onto the first one. In summer all the slaves happily take off their shoes and go barefoot.

In a small building next to the shoe shop two women dip candles. The spinsters make thick linen wicks for them. The candlemakers cut these twice as long as a candle. They hang a wick across a rod and twist its two ends together. When the rod has five wicks spaced a little on it, a woman takes it by both ends and dips the wicks into a pot of melted tallow. She puts the rod across a rack and lets the tallow cool and harden. Then she dips the wicks again, and again. Each dipping and cooling adds a new layer and soon she has five candles hanging on the rod. These will be used in the Big House and in the overseers' houses. If the slaves need light in their cabins, they burn a cruse just like the one the oronooko used.

School hours at Shaw's Fortune are whenever Oliver Bennett is free from his other work: usually before breakfast, from six to ten. Tom and Ellen like it better when it is between breakfast and dinner; then they can ride with their father in the morning. Oliver is a better teacher than Giles Watson was. Giles could read and do simple "sums," but Oliver went to Harvard College in Massachusetts.

The schoolroom couldn't hold more than ten children but that is all right, since only five, and sometimes six, children use it. Tom and Ellen study here. So does Will Woodruff, the son of Carrie and Amos. Will is a year younger than Tom and they are good friends. The manager's twin sons, Henry and Stephen Davis, are also pupils. The sixth pupil is Lucy. She likes to come for an hour now and then and study her letters with the others. Next year she will come every day.

The schoolroom's two windows give little light. On dark winter days Mr. Bennett has to light candles. He sits beside a small table, in a straight-backed armchair, facing the children. They sit on long benches that have no backs at all. Each bench has a low table in front of it. This schoolroom has no blackboard and paper is too scarce to use for school work, so the children write on slates. These actually are made of smoothed slate set in a wooden frame to keep it from breaking. The slates are about as big as a page of this book. Pencils made of softer slate make whitish marks on them. A damp cloth takes the marks off.

The school is really for Tom. He will someday run the plantation, so he has to learn. Ellen is now reading a book called *The Governess, or the Little Female Academy*. She also practices writing and studies plain arithmetic. The "three R's" are all a lady needs to know. But Ellen is also learning to spin, to weave, to sew, to knit, and many other things that will help her to run her own house someday.

Will, Henry, and Stephen come to the school, too, but they will not go much further with lessons than Ellen will. They haven't caught up with her yet because they started later. The twins are still struggling with the *New England Primer*.

Tom studies English and Latin grammar and practices writing "a clear running hand." He has taken Latin for five years and can now read it almost as fast as he reads English. For the last two years Oliver has been teaching him Greek. Tom has gone beyond plain arithmetic into "accompts" (bookkeeping) and surveying. He also studies geography and history, English history of course. Nobody bothers about American history yet.

Tom's Latin book belongs to his grandfather. It has a brown leather cover. Ellen's reader has a cardboard cover with blue paper pasted on it. The twins' American primer is covered with thin wood which also has blue paper on it. Lucy has a "hornbook." It isn't really a book at all. It is a wooden paddle with a small sheet of paper on it. The alphabet is printed on the paper in large letters. A polished split of cow horn, thin enough to see through, protects the paper.

*Hornbook*

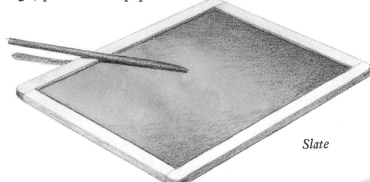

*Slate*

*Catching soft crabs*

*Lucy's hoop*

*Ellen's doll*

The children at Shaw's Fortune have plenty of fun. When the tobacco ship comes to the plantation wharf, Oliver Bennett's whole school spends every free minute on it or near it. Sometimes they sail around it in Tom's little skiff. It is fun to fish from the skiff for "croakers" and perch. The boys also wade in shallow water and catch soft crabs with hand nets. They tow a washtub along and stow their catch in it.

In the fall Tom and Will and the twins, and sometimes Ellen, too, follow the fox hunt. Their small horses can't jump the high fences that the gentlemen get over, so they dash from hill to hill and try to keep the hounds and the riders in sight. Sometimes they get a glimpse of the fox.

The children have few toys. Lucy rolls a hoop. It is taller than she is and was made to fit around a tobacco cask. Ellen has a wooden doll that the ship's captain brought to her from London. It doesn't look like a baby; it looks like a grown woman and is dressed in silk. The boys whip tops on the paved walk in front of the Big House. They start them spinning by wrapping the lash of a small whip on them and then unwinding it with a quick pull. The trick is to keep the top spinning by stroking it with the whiplash.

The boys also pitch horseshoes. The stablemen have set pins by the lane and there are plenty of old shoes to toss at them. When they are not working, the slave boys join in the games.

Sometimes it is tipcat, which they play just as boys play it now, with sticks for bats and a short wooden cat, sharpened at both ends. With the cat in a ring on the ground, they bring the bat down on one end of it. This makes the cat jump into the air and the batter swings at it quickly, before it can fall. He can knock it some distance. The other players try to catch it. If they can throw it into the ring, the batter is "out."

Ellen sometimes joins the boys for a game of bowls. They all love this game. The bowls are too heavy for them, so they play with their own rules. The dark wooden bowls and the "jack" belong to their father. He and his friends play on the lawn, which is far from smooth enough for a real bowling green. The game looks easy but it isn't. The white jack, a ball half as big as the others, lies on the green. The two teams bowl at it. They try to get their bowls as close to it as they can. They may knock their own team's bowls closer to the jack, or the other team's away from it. What makes it hard is that the bowls are not round balls. They are made a little lopsided on purpose.

On rainy days Ellen and Tom play indoor games: "draughts," which we call checkers; backgammon, played on a double board with dice and counters; and piquet, a card game for two, using only the thirty-two highest cards. Sometimes Tom plays chess with his grandfather.

*Tipcat*

*Bowls*

Six of the horses in the family stable are white. They pull the coach but they are also used for other work. Malcolm Shaw has two fine riding horses, one black and one chestnut. Miss Sally rides a quiet mare named Dolly. Tom's Punch and Ellen's Judy are stabled here, too. They are large ponies and, like their owners, they are brother and sister. The old horse that works in the garden and pulls Mose's wagon lives in this stable, too.

The carriage house, across the lane from the stable, has Mose's wagon in it, and Malcolm's gig. This is a two-wheeled cart pulled by one horse. It has a folding leather top that can be raised in bad weather. Next to the gig is the coachee. Two horses pull it, and it carries six people and a driver. The passengers enter it at the back and sit on two lengthwise seats. The coachee's top can't be folded, but it has leather curtains that roll up on bright days.

The last, the largest, and the most important vehicle in the carriage house is the coach. It came from London twenty years ago, lashed to the deck of a tobacco ship, but its blue paint and gilt are as bright as when Duncan bought it. Brutus keeps it covered with big sheets. Its hind wheels are large, and its front wheels are very small. The body sways between them, hang-

ing on thick leather straps. This coach has no springs at all. Its passengers sit on cushioned seats which face each other. They look out through windows of French plate glass.

Today is Sunday. The Shaws ate an early breakfast and, except for Lucy who is staying home, they are dressed in their best clothes to go to church. Brutus sits on his high seat. He wears his blue and gold livery coat, his white wig, and his black three-cornered hat. His hands hold four reins and a long-lashed whip. The reins control the four horses nearest to him. His son, Tony, guides the leading pair of horses and rides on the left-hand one. Caesar, acting as footman, is holding the

coach door open. As soon as the family is seated, he will close it and get up on a small platform between the back wheels. He rides standing on this and holding on to two loops attached to the edge of the coach roof.

Lucy and Pompey watch from the front doorstep. Amanda and Leonidas watch from the kitchen door. Brutus cracks his whip and speaks to his horses, Tony speaks to his, too, and the coach lumbers off. The church is nine miles away. Pompey wonders whether the Shaws will have dinner at some other plantation, or will bring friends back here for dinner. He and Amanda have to be ready for anything.

## ABOUT THE AUTHOR

EDWIN TUNIS, well-known artist, illustrator, and muralist, was born at Cold Spring Harbor, N.Y. He is now living in Maryland, writing and painting. His articles have appeared in various magazines and he has exhibited at the Baltimore Museum of Art, Society of American Etchers, National Academy of Design, Victoria and Albert Museum, and other well-known galleries. His most ambitious art project was a mural depicting the History of Spices, which is 145 feet long and took two and a half years to paint. The many ancient ships in this painting required much research and prompted Mr. Tunis to write *Oars, Sails and Steam*, the first of his fine pictorial histories. This was followed by *Weapons* and, later, by *Wheels*.

Mr. Tunis' special interest in American history has resulted in a distinguished group of books depicting many aspects of this country's past: *Colonial Craftsmen: And the Beginnings of American Industry; Colonial Living; Frontier Living;* and *Indians. Shaw's Fortune* is the first of several planned picture-story books for younger readers, showing and telling in brief texts and many beautiful drawings what life in America was like in earlier days.

1   2   3   4   5   70   69   68   67   66